A word from the editor

The purpose of *The Jargon Buster* is to open the language of adult learning to all. Acronyms and professional terms, sometimes used as a kind of shorthand by those 'in the know' can create barriers to newcomers (and even experienced practitioners) entering the world of adult learning.

This edition of *The Jargon Buster* covers the most common terms that practitioners are likely to come across in books, articles, reports, evaluations and government papers, with regard to adult learning in England and Wales. It is not intended to be exhaustive but starts with the most frequently used terms and those which are most confusing.

It should be noted that terminology, structures and initiatives in the post-compulsory learning field often have a limited life. It is necessary to be updated at regular intervals. The definitions in *The Jargon Buster* have been contributed by many colleagues within NIACE and gleaned from a variety of written sources. I am deeply indebted to everyone for their assistance and contributions. In each case I have identified the term, added an acronym where applicable, provided a definition and in some cases suggested linked terms that readers might wish to refer to.

Yanina Dutton

Foreword

The conceptual language used in the field of adult education and learning often gets in the way of real understanding and thinking by becoming over-jargonized and acronym-heavy. Having changed occupation several times, I have been forced to learn a new 'language' every time. As a Norwegian I have noticed this especially when travelling abroad, mostly to English-speaking countries. You may not know this, but the English language is much richer than the Nordic languages and, as such, is filled with many more synonyms and acronyms. Coming to England to work at NIACE for six months in 2003, all the acronyms, names and new words I encountered, became like an alphabet soup to me. I should really have had *The Jargon Buster* then!

The world of adult education is like any other profession; it has its own vocabulary, terminology, acronyms, synonyms, and jargon. This seems to be important to policy makers and practitioners alike: to defend us against outsiders; to shelter ourselves from the winds of challenge; and also to secure precision and exactness in our mission. We need terminology to be accurate, correct, exact, distinct and precise in our communication. But sometimes we go too far. As the work we do grows and widens, both nationally and internationally, we increasingly meet colleagues not (yet) familiar with our selection of words – our jargon.

The purpose of *The Jargon Buster* is to be a little helper to us all – both new and old – professional and voluntary workers in the field of adult education, adult learning, further and continuing education, adult and community learning, lifelong and life-wide learning (and yes of course, you will find these different terms explained in this book!). You will also be able to check out your understanding of important terms and hopefully make better sense of all the professional correspondence you regularly receive.

Dig into this publication and explore and learn for yourselves.

Sturla Bjerkaker
Visiting Director NIACE February – August 2003
Director of the Norwegian Association for Adult Education
Board member of the European Association for the Education of Adults

F

The Jargon Buster

Uni
Subj

htt

E.
P!

Compiled by
Yanina Dutton

Published by the National Institute of
Adult Continuing Education (England and Wales)

21 De Montfort Street
Leicester LE1 7GE
Company registration no. 2603322
Charity registration no. 1002775

First published 2005

The *NIACE lifelines in adult learning series* is supported by the Adult
and Community Learning Fund. ACLF is funded by the Department
for Education and Skills and managed in partnership by NIACE and
the Basic Skills Agency to develop widening participation in adult learning.

promoting adult learning

NIACE has a broad remit to promote lifelong learning
opportunities for adults. NIACE works to develop
increased participation in education and training,
particularly for those who do not have easy access
because of barriers of class, gender, age, race,
language and culture, learning difficulties and
disabilities, or insufficient financial resources.

www.niace.org.uk

Cataloguing in Publication Data
A CIP record of this title is available from the British Library

Designed and typeset by Boldface
Printed in Great Britain by Russell Press, Nottingham

ISBN 1 86201 215 6

A

A/AS Levels

These are academic qualifications. First introduced in 1951 and most recently updated in 2000. They are intended to be taken when learners are 17 and 18, though may adult learners also take them. Younger learners now take 4 or 5 Advanced Supplementary (AS) Levels when they are 17, and then take 2, 3 or 4 of their preferred subjects onto A Level, usually at the age of 18.

Access

In an adult education context, access is a generic term that embraces the various factors that affect a person's ability to take advantage of organised education and training provision. These include issues relating to the location and timing of courses; the physical accessibility of venues and the nature of support provided for people with disabilities; the costs, both direct (fees) and indirect (transport, books, equipment, childcare), of participation; the conditions for entry to a programme e.g. whether certain levels of qualification are required, and the cultural and intellectual appropriateness of the curriculum for different groups of learners.

Improving conditions of access should be the first stage in any strategy to increase and widen adult participation in learning. (See widening participation.)

Access courses

Access courses (with a small 'a') generally refer to preparatory courses or programmes that have been designed to help adults return to learning or to a certain level of learning. Access courses/ programmes (with a capital 'A') are those that have been specifically designed to prepare adult learners without A-Level qualifications for entry to higher education. Usually offered in further education and adult residential colleges, these have proved particularly attractive to women and members of ethnic minority communities. In recent years they have become increasingly oriented towards vocational subjects such as health studies, social work and nursing.

Access funds

These are funds allocated by Government to enable further and higher education institutions to assist the participation of students who have difficulties with meeting the expenses and living costs involved in studying. In further education access funds can include the costs of childcare. In higher education Access and Hardship Funds include Opportunity Bursaries and fee waivers for part-time students. The Government is simplifying financial support for students in higher education, especially those with dependants and those with disabilities. A new Access to Learning Fund began in 2004.

Accreditation
There are three possible definitions of this term:

1) The process through which the regulatory authorities, such as the Qualifications and Curriculum Authority (QCA), confirm that a *qualification and associated specification* conform to the relevant accreditation criteria.
2) The process through which an awarding body confirms that a programme or course leading to an award is of sufficient quality to meet the relevant accreditation criteria for that programme. In this definition, which describes the process used by Open College Networks and many other awarding bodies, it is the *programme or course* that is the object accredited, not the qualification. Although this definition has no statutory authority, it is the one more widely used in the post-school sector than the one developed by the Qualifications and Curriculum Authority.
3) The recognition of achievement by a learner through the award of credit. Although this is the most literal definition of *accreditation*, and the one which conforms most closely to definitions used outside the learning and skills sector (e.g. in journalism), it is rarely used in this way by awarding bodies.

Thus the object of accreditation may be a qualification (1) or a programme (2) but is rarely a learner (3). (See Open College Network; Qualifications and Curriculum Authority.)

Accreditation of prior experiential learning (APEL)
The process through which the previously uncertificated achievements of an individual (in the home, at work or in unpaid voluntary activity) are formally recognised in the context of an award. APEL is explicitly related to previously uncertificated achievements.

Accreditation of prior learning (APL)
The distinction between APEL and APL has arisen through the incorrect use of the term APL to describe the process of exemption – i.e. the 'counting' of previously *certificated* achievement towards the requirements of another award. In fact the two terms are identical in their usage.

Action on Access
This is the national co-ordination team appointed by the Higher Education Funding Council for England (HEFCE) and the Learning & Skills Council (LSC) to support their Widening Participation strategies for England. The team also supports the Department of Employment and Learning, Northern Ireland (DELNI) in Widening Participation. The team supports the Aimhigher: Partnerships for Progression (P4P)

initiative funded jointly by the HEFCE and the LSC. Action on Access works with further and higher education institutions and supports individual institutions with their widening participation strategies. The team undertakes commissioned research and influences and contributes to the policies of the funding councils.

Action plans

Action plans are the written commitments that individuals and organisations draw up to ensure that they are working towards their goals and targets. They record dates, actions and responsibilities and can be used in reviews with line managers to monitor progress. They can be modified in the light of developments. In the context of adult learning, action plans are usually negotiated between tutors and learners at the start of a programme.

Action research

Action research is a type of research in which the researcher is also an agent of change and part of the process of change. The researcher together with the subjects of the research are asked to take part in a sequenced process which involves research (investigating a problem and presenting an initial analysis with one or more proposed solutions); followed by action (deciding which course of action to follow and then pursuing it); followed by further research (further investigation to assess what happens, including anything unexpected together with possible solutions and adjustments); followed by further action (to refine the policies or ways of working which are being developed). The process can continue indefinitely as the original focus of concern extends into new areas. (See Participatory Learning Appraisal.)

Action Zones

Action Zones are areas of deprivation identified by central Government initiatives for specific funding to encourage partnership and project working with disadvantaged groups. Examples include Employment, Health and Education Action Zones. They have been linked to other area-based initiatives (e.g. Sure Start) through planning in Local Strategic Partnerships. (See Education Action Zone; Health Action Zone; Local Strategic Partnerships.)

Activation of Prior Knowledge

Activation of Prior Knowledge is an instructional strategy that aims to help students to become independent in activating their own prior knowledge. Research on prior knowledge has shown that students construct meaning by using their prior knowledge to interact with a text. A thematic organization in which themes are carefully developed with related pieces of literature also supports the activation and development of prior knowledge; by reading several related selections, students build on their prior knowledge from previous selections as they read the next selection.

Active citizenship
Active citizenship encourages people to get involved personally, practically and politically in local or national affairs and in articulating and pursuing their concerns. Active citizenship is the practice of being directly and actively involved in government, national or local politics or matters affecting the welfare of others and society as a whole. To be an active citizen can also include being a caring neighbour, a volunteer and someone who reports crime. (See citizenship; citizenship education.)

Active Community Unit
The Active Community Unit is a unit in the Home Office which promotes the development of the voluntary and community sector and to encourage people to become actively involved in their communities, particularly in deprived areas.

Added value (or value added)
In a learning context, added value usually refers to the incremental personal and social achievements as well as the intellectual and skills gains made by learners on completion of a programme, compared with their possession of these attributes on entry.

Additionality
Additionality represents the value added to a project, plan or organization by a new resource. This must be a new resource not double-funding or the replication of something that is already happening.

Adult and community learning
This term entered common usage when the Adult and Community Learning Fund (ACLF) was launched in 1998, however, there is no universally accepted definition. The term is used to refer to:

- a *sector* (as distinct from further education, higher education);
- the kinds of *programmes* typically delivered by some providers (Local Education Authorities (LEAs), the Workers Education Association (WEA) and other voluntary sector bodies), some of which are accredited;
- any form of *non-accredited adult education*;
- a particular (informal and flexible) *approach to learning for adults*;
- a *funding stream* (Adult Community Learning Fund (ACLF); the Learning and Skills Council (LSC) budget head for some provision delivered by LEAs), or to *informal, community-based learning activities* of the kind funded by ACLF.

In policy documents, the term now usually refers to the non-accredited learning provision funded by the LSC and delivered mainly by LEAs.

Adult and Community Learning Fund (ACLF)

The Adult and Community Learning Fund was launched by the DfES in 1998 as part of a national strategy to widen participation in learning and improve levels of literacy and numeracy among the adult population. The fund, which ran until March 2004, was a programme of small (up to £10k per annum) and major (up to £30k per annum) grants available to organisations working with adults in England. It aimed to investigate and develop what works in widening participation, opening access to learning, developing basic skills, building the capacity of community-based providers and supporting effective partnerships. The LSC has launched the Widening Adult Participation Action Fund (WAPAF) which replaced the ACLF in 2004.

Adult (and community) learning practitioners

Adult learning practitioners are the people who work with adults either in educational settings (adult education institutions, further education colleges, university adult education, schools) or in community settings (such as community and health centres, clubs, sports venues). The term can include teachers, outreach workers, guidance workers, organisers and people working in a variety of other roles involving engagement with adults learning.

Adult education

Adult education was until the 1990s the general umbrella term used to cover the range of daytime and evening, formal and non-formal, part-time or full-time, education provision available for adults who had completed their initial education. It embraced all skills and branches of knowledge. The term is often narrowly applied just to the courses provided by local education authorities and the Workers Education Association (WEA), although further and higher education institutions also provide a significant amount of adult education. To some extent the term has been superseded by 'Adult Learning' or 'Adult and Community Learning'. (See adult and community learning.)

Adult education practitioners – see adult (and community) learning practitioners.

Adult learners

The term usually refers to people who engage in education and training after a gap has occurred since completion of their initial education, as opposed to those who stay on after school to enter mainstream further or higher education that are usually described as 'students'. The use of the adjective 'adult' however is problematic. National participation surveys tend to treat anyone from age 17 as adult learners (including those who are in full-time education) while educational policy tends to differentiate between 'young people' (16-19) and 'adults' (19+). The term 'learner' is also problematic, in that learners rarely describe themselves as such and it is much more likely to be a term used by professionals *about* those on the receiving end of education.

Adult Learners' Forum

A meeting of adult learners currently involved in education, who meet together to offer support, share experiences, identify issues and concerns and to campaign for improvements.

Adult Learners' Week

Adult Learners' Week is a promotional campaign established in the UK by NIACE in 1992 to raise the profile of adult learning. The campaign aims to widen access to learning opportunities and to encourage more people to seek advice and guidance about returning to learn. The Week, co-ordinated by NIACE, now has its equivalent in more than 40 countries worldwide.

Adult Learning Inspectorate (ALI)

The ALI is the government body responsible for raising the standards of education and training for adults in England by inspecting and reporting on the quality of learning provision they receive. The Inspectorate was established by the Education and Skills Act 2000. Its remit covers:

- work-based training for all people over the age of 16
- education for people aged over 19 in further education colleges
- all adult and community learning
- e-learning via Learndirect provided by the University for Industry
- employment training funded by Jobcentre Plus, including New Deal
- learning in prisons
- training provided by private industry at the employer's invitation

Adult Learning Plans

Local authorities are required to produce an Adult Learning Plan against which funding is allocated by the Local Learning and Skills Council (LLSC). In preparing these Plans, authorities have the opportunity to build on their existing learning plans and to take advantage of new opportunities offered through the Learning and Skills Council (LSC). Whilst ensuring that there is a strong focus on widening participation and on helping local people to overcome disadvantage, in finalising their plans Local Education Authorities are also expected to show how they intend to meet the needs of local people who are already committed to learning. LLSCs are responsible for the approval of Adult Learning Plans for their area and these documents are available to the public.

Advanced Modern Apprenticeship (AMA) – see Modern Apprenticeships.

Advocacy
Advocacy is the process of supporting and enabling people, especially those experiencing disadvantage, such as students with learning difficulties, to express their views and concerns; to access information and services; to defend and promote their rights; and to explore choices and options. Advocates support and argue the case for service users and assist the users in putting across their point of view. Advocacy can influence outcomes, including public policy and resource allocation decisions that directly affect people's lives.

Aimhigher
Aimhigher is the brand name for the Government's initiative to achieve 50% of young people (18-30) participating in higher education. It also aims to increase participation from the social groups that are currently under-represented in higher education.

Androgogy
The term was developed by Malcolm Knowles in the USA in the 1980s. Andragogy is the adult counterpart of pedagogy. It refers to the process of teaching adults as distinct from teaching children.

Anti-discriminatory practice
Involves working with individuals and groups in ways that celebrate diversity but takes an explicit stand against oppression, discrimination and prejudice.

Appraisal
Appraisal in an educational context can refer to:

• the process of assessing a grant application before a decision is taken
• the formal review of the performance of a member of staff

(See evaluation.)

Assessment is a process often involving written or oral examinations or course-work through which a learner's achievements are measured according to specified criteria. There are many types of assessments, including:

- continuous – regular evaluation of coursework, where the marks achieved count towards the final result.
- formative – a way of determining a person's strengths and weaknesses with the objective of improving them. This is generally expressed in words rather than grades, and usually not used in the final assessment.
- convergent – the emphasis is restricted to the ability of the students to focus upon a clearly defined task.
- group – the group as a whole, rather than each member of the group, is given a common mark.
- individual – each learner, even if involved in group work, is assessed separately.
- peer – assessment is undertaken by a fellow (peer) learner or fellow professional in the discipline.
- ipsative – assessment is measured against the prior performance of the person being assessed. For example, in athletics, measuring a result against 'personal best' is an example of ipsative assessment.
- summative – takes place towards the end of a course or programme. It can lead to the attribution of a grade or a mark which completes the course or which allows the learner to move to the next part or level of the course.

Asylum seeker/refugee

Whilst often referred to as a single group, asylum seekers and refugees are in reality a diverse range of people from different cultures, countries and communities. The term asylum seeker applies to those people who have applied for asylum and whose applications are under consideration or those who have received a refusal but have not yet returned to their home country. The term refugee applies to a person who, having applied for asylum has been given "recognised refugee status", "exceptional leave to remain" or "indefinite leave to remain" in the UK. There are important differences in the legal rights of asylum seekers and refugees which impact upon their access to education, training and employment.

B

Barriers to learning

The barriers to learning are the structural, situational or dispositional factors that act as obstacles to a person's engagement in organised learning. These may include, a lack of suitable learning opportunities or opportunities at times and in locations that suit individuals (structural barriers); caring or work responsibilities (situational barriers), feeling too old to learn or anxiety about ones ability to learn (dispositional barriers).

Basic skills

Basic skills are those skills needed to read, write and speak in English and use mathematics, at a level necessary to function at work and in society in general. In the 2003 skills strategy ICT was designated as a fourth basic skill. (See *Skills for Life*.) Increasingly, professionals working in this area prefer not to use the term 'basic skills' because they think it sounds insulting. They talk about literacy, language and numeracy skills or 'skills for life'.

Benchmark

A benchmark is an accepted standard of service or achievement that is established as a means of ensuring comparable standards across a system or field of activity. It allows the measurement of the impact or success of an activity or process by comparing it against something similar. Benchmarking indicates the factors which make a process or activity effective, and informs future performance as part of quality assurance.

Best Value

Best Value is a performance framework applied to local authority services. Each local authority is required to review each of its services in turn over a four year cycle, to consider whether the service should continue, where and how it needs to improve or change, and to report on the recommendations and outcomes to the public. Most reviews are undertaken by a small panel of local government officers and elected members (councillors) and led by an officer nominated from another department within the local authority, than the one being reviewed. The reviews are usually conducted in line with a standard process developed by each local authority from national guidance. The Best Value process is based on what are referred to as the four Cs – challenge, compare, compete and consult. Local authorities are inspected to ensure that the review processes they apply are sufficiently rigorous.

Bite-sized

Bite-sized is the term used to describe small, manageable pieces of learning which are considered to be appropriate for new and less experienced learners. The Learning and Skills Council has funded local authorities to deliver bite-sized learning experiences to engage new groups of learners.

Blended learning

Blended learning is a term used to describe the method of integrating traditional learning methods with on-line-learning. It can involve the classroom and the

Internet, as well as traditional paper and books and allows students to learn at their own pace. There is no preferred blended learning method. Certain courses are best taught in the classroom, whereas others can be taught almost wholly online.

Board of trustees
A Board of Trustees is a group of people who are responsible in law for the running of a charity. They can also be called a Management Committee, an Executive Committee, a Board of Directors or a Council.

The trustees should not benefit from their position (though they may be users of the organisation's services). Whilst trustees who provide professional services (lawyers who provide legal advice, for example) may be paid for the specific service, trustees are not normally paid. Members of staff can advise the board but they cannot be trustees themselves.

Bottom-up
This phrase is applied to decisions or developments that originate not with professionals or people in higher decision-making roles (a '*top-down*' approach) but with people whom they involve on the ground. Many believe that bottom-up developments are more likely to have an impact as they are owned and supported by those they most affect.

C

Capacity building
Capacity-building involves development work and activities that strengthen the ability of an organisation or community to build skills, structures and solutions. It is often used in relation to helping local groups to take part in the social and economic regeneration of their area by developing their skills and confidence, setting up and strengthening networks, and improving organisation and procedures. It also applies to the training and development of workers and volunteers in order to fulfil their organisational objectives.

Capital Funding
Capital Funding is finance made available specifically for the purchase or improvement of fixed assets such as premises or equipment.

Careers Guidance
Careers Guidance is the practice of advising people about opportunities and openings in employment. It connects to Educational Guidance in the sense that people

need to be aware of the necessary entry level qualifications and skills for their prospective careers or chosen jobs. It is offered by specialists in education organisations or by specialist privatised providers.

Centres of Vocational Excellence (COVEs)

These are further education centres specialising in a range of vocational fields (e.g. engineering, health and social care, construction). The initiative was launched in July 2002 in 16 pathfinder centres. The objectives are: to develop and strengthen innovative approaches by colleges and providers to meeting the country's skills needs; to enhance the standing of Learning and Skills Council-funded providers with employers; to encourage collaboration and to promote the concept of excellence in economically-relevant specialisms.

The national target is for 400 COVEs to be established by 2006 and to have extended them beyond colleges to training centres in companies and other training providers.

Certification

Certification refers to the process whereby knowledge, skills and competencies are recognised through provision of a formal document to learners who have success-fully completed a course or module of study. Certification can also involve the formal recognition of prior knowledge and skills.

Citizenship

Citizenship refers to the rights and duties of individuals who are residents and members of a nation state. In Britain, citizenship has three elements: civil (civil rights are necessary for individual freedoms and should be recognised and safeguarded by the law); political (the right to participate in political activities such as demonstrating, lobbying, voting or holding political office); and social (the right to experience a decent standard of living and quality of life as embodied in the welfare, educational and cultural systems of society).

The notion of citizenship implies personal agency and social engagement, and in some cases the achievement of citizenship rights through social struggle. This is rather different from the notions of citizenship which are 'handed down from above' or 'tested' by the government of the day. (See active citizenship; citizenship education.)

Citizenship education

Refers to educational programmes and activities designed to prepare people for their roles as citizens in a changing society. The content of such programmes is contentious: it could be concerned with securing conservative understandings of 'good behaviour' and social participation especially by those who are considered problematic to society in some way; or it could be concerned with encouraging a more radical understanding of active citizenship, especially in the interests of those social groups who are least powerful in society. (See active citizenship; citizenship.)

Citizens' Panels

These are panels of people operating at local level who are usually representative of the population as a whole and who are specially chosen to deliberate on complex social issues. Panels hear expert evidence and can call witnesses in order to form their views. Citizens' Panels demonstrate how people with little formal knowledge of an issue, can handle complex evidence and reach complex conclusions when given opportunities to question experts, form judgements and make recommendations.

City Challenge

City Challenge was a five-year Government initiative, launched in 1991 and now completed. It aimed to transform specific rundown inner city areas and significantly improve the quality of life for local residents within the target area.

Collaborative browsing

Collaborative browsing is a software-enabled technique that allows people to surf the web together. In a learning situation one person (student or teacher) can take the other person around different web sites.

Collaborative learning

This is an instructional method in which participants work together in small groups towards a common goal. The learners may be mutually responsible for each other's learning.

Colloquium

This is a conference or seminar for academic or other specialists, where research papers are delivered and discussed, and the whole is often published in a book or electronic form, as a contribution to knowledge of the specialist subject.

Common Inspection Framework

This is the framework used by both the Adult Learning Inspectorate (ALI) and the Office for Standards in Education (OfSTED) that sets out details of how to inspect and evaluate post-compulsory education and training outside the higher education sector. The aim is to keep the Secretary of State for Education and Skills informed about the quality of education and training and the standards achieved by students. The Common Inspection Framework focuses on learners, learning and the impact of learning. (See Adult Learning Inspectorate; Ofsted.)

Community

The word 'community' has become contentious in recent years as it is used loosely despite its range of potential meanings. For example it can be understood in any of the following ways:

- *as a geographical community*: people living in a particular area – a street, an estate, a village, a town or a larger space
- *as an interest community*: a group sharing a common interest (e.g. clubs, societies, political parties, religious faiths)
- *as an occupational community*: people working in similar fields
- *as a cultural community*: for example, people sharing an ethnic or social class background.

All of these imply a sense of belonging and identity and a sharing of concerns.

The word 'community' generally implies something that is positive and desirable and it is often appended to policies and developments with the intention of creating a positive approach. When applied to education, the term has connotations of accessibility, especially in terms of location.

Community Chest

Community Chest is a funding mechanism to encourage and support community activity, as a first step in enabling more people in deprived areas to become involved in the regeneration of their communities. Community Chests help community groups get started by funding small purchases, such as buying toys for a local playgroup, funding a community outing, or hiring a meeting space. The grants are made available by the Neighbourhood Renewal Unit as part of the National Strategy for Neighbourhood Renewal and are restricted to the 88 Neighbourhood Renewal pilot areas. The grants are administered through regional Government Offices.

Community cohesion

Community cohesion is about helping different communities work together to achieve a shared view of the future, greater respect for differences in culture, background and outlook, and ways of dealing with local issues. The idea, which is now an area of government policy, stems from concern about the potential for distrust, hostility and violence between communities that live side-by-side but do not have any real contact or understanding of each other, and which are also struggling with poverty, neglect, discrimination and racism.

Creative consultation

Creative consultation is an approach to consulting with local people that sets out to ensure their views feed directly into the decisions that affect their lives. It helps people work towards lasting answers in new and imaginative ways. It starts from where learners and citizens are and gives them a central role in deciding and taking action to achieve change. Along with community development work, creative consultation is based on the ideas of partnership, involving everyone and shifting power towards those who have it least.

Community development
Community development is a process which involves working with people in neighbourhoods and communities to increase levels of self-help, support and collective action. It aims to give people greater control over their communities and individual situations.

Community development can cover projects and services intended to provide practical benefits to an area, for example improved social services, more relevant vocational training, and job creation schemes. The underlying idea is to find new and imaginative solutions to problems and make better use of existing resources. Key features of community development include:

- participation
- empowerment
- positive action/new opportunities
- partnership

Community education
Community education is a way of working with people through learning in the places where they live and in response to the interests, issues and aspirations that are important to them. This sometimes involves formal learning but is much more likely to involve a mix of non-formal and informal learning. It is often associated with the delivery of organised educational programmes in an outreach environment. (See formal learning; informal learning; non-formal learning.)

Community Empowerment Fund (CEF)
This is a government-initiated fund intended to help community and voluntary groups to become empowered in order to participate in Local Strategic Partnerships and neighbourhood renewal. Government Offices for the Regions are responsible for distributing CEF resources and there is £60m from 2001-2006. (See local strategic partnerships, neighbourhood renewal.)

Community Forum
This is the national body with experience of regeneration and poverty issues that advises the Neighbourhood Renewal Unit on how to ensure that community groups

and residents are able to play an inclusive and effective role in neighbourhood renewal. (See neighbourhood renewal.)

Community Fund

The Community Fund is the operating name of the National Lottery Charities Board, which distributes national lottery money to charities and voluntary organisations for specific projects. The final awards grants for initiatives that help meet the needs of those at greatest disadvantage and to improve the quality of life in society. The fund merged with the New Opportunity Fund in 2004 to become The Big Lottery Fund.

Community groups

Community groups are people from specific communities, locations or ethnic groups, who may or may not have shared interests or goals. In an educational context, the term is often used to refer to diverse groups residing or working in any given location.

Community mapping

Community mapping is an approach involving techniques and methods to identify the different groups who live or work in any given location. It can be conducted by organisations and outreach workers in order to know where to target services.

It can also involve community residents who participate in analysing their own access barriers to something of importance, such as looking at different types of adult learning courses available in the local area. Assistance is given from local workers and policy makers who are in a position to make positive changes. A local action plan is then established outlining the findings of the mapping exercise and the actions that local people have identified as necessary for things to improve.

Community plan

Local authorities are required to develop community plans for improvement of the economic, environmental and social well being of local areas. Through these plans authorities are expected to co-ordinate the actions of local public, private, voluntary and community organisations. Community plans are designed to improve the delivery and quality of services in local authority areas. In the neighbourhood renewal pilot areas the responsibility for compiling the community plan belongs to Local Strategic Partnerships. (See local strategic partnerships; neighbourhood renewal.)

Community regeneration

This is a process of helping particular neighbourhoods or communities that have experienced poverty, de-industrialisation, unemployment, low educational achievements and other disadvantages, to work towards improving their own environment and creating new social, cultural, educational, civic and economic structures and activities.

Community-based learning

Community-based learning is based on what local people want to learn. This type of learning is provided locally, such as in community halls, schools, football clubs, health centres, pubs, and on buses that take learning out to remote areas. It deals directly with barriers to learning such as poverty and family responsibilities by providing childcare, help with transport and lower fees or free courses. Community-based learning offers people who would not dare to enter formal education the chance to enjoy stimulating and high-quality learning in their own neighbourhood.

Compact

This is an agreement between two or more parties setting out how they will work together to achieve common aims. Unlike a contract which is binding in law, a compact is usually a statement of good intent and co-operation. It is frequently used to describe a working agreement between schools and/or sixth form colleges with higher education institutions which aims to familiarise students with the higher education environment. More recently the term has been developed to underpin the working relationships between government departments and the various bodies with whom they work.

Competences (sometimes spelt as competencies)

In a training and employment context, these refer to specific job-related skills and the proven ability to perform certain tasks required in a job or as part of a vocational qualification.

Computer-based learning

This is an interactive instructional approach in which the computer takes the place of an instructor, providing information and questions or exercises, as well as feedback to the learner's responses.

Computer conferencing

Discussions between groups of participants in different places using computer networks to transmit text messages. If this is done by simple email, it may be through the use of a list server. Computer conferencing has become a standard part of distance learning courses run through the Internet. (See open learning and distance learning.)

Connexions

Connexions is the central government programme that aims to provide a range of guidance and support for 13 to 19 year olds in order to help them with issues such as careers, health, relationships, housing, education and money. It aims to provide integrated advice, guidance and access to personal development opportunities via telephone, e-mail, web chat and text messaging, as well as face-to-face meetings. Every young person in England should have access to a personal advisor through local partnerships.

Contingency funds

This refers to money put to one side to cover unanticipated costs or emergencies.

Continuing education (CE)

Continuing education is used to refer to any education undertaken by an adult after completing compulsory education. The term has largely been replaced by 'life long learning', although it has survived in universities where it refers particularly to continuing professional development.

Continuing Professional Development (CPD)

This is a type of continuing education for specific professions. It aims to keep skills and knowledge up-to-date and is compulsory in many professions, such as medicine, law and engineering. CPD tends to offer higher education credit, usually at postgraduate (masters) level. CPD is commonly delivered as short intensive courses from one to three days, and not always on a university campus.

Core skills

Core skills are defined as those skills which are common to a wide range of tasks and are essential for competence in those tasks. They are categorised under four headings: number and its application, communication, problem-solving and practical skills. These four areas were chosen specifically to support the development of a technically competent workforce.

Credit

Credit refers to the award that is made to a learner in recognition of the verified achievement of designated learning outcomes at a specified level.

Credit accumulation and transfer scheme or system (CATS)

This is a scheme or system that permits learners to accumulate credits towards a named award, and to transfer these credits (under certain conditions) to other awards that are part of the same credit scheme or system. The original use of the term CATS was developed in relation to its use solely in the context of higher education. Recently it has been applied more generally to any functioning credit system. The implementation of a CATS scheme should enable students to accumulate and transfer credits across different institutions.

Critical thinking

Critical thinking encourages a questioning approach to learning, including information handling and the ability to make reasoned arguments supported by evidence.

Cultural capital

This is a term originally used by Pierre Bourdieu to describe the way in which middle-class children learn from their background and families of origin, various linguistic and cultural competences (for example, familiarity with books or music and what constitutes 'appropriate behaviour' and 'manners' in social situations). These are the kinds of competences which are pre-requisites for educational success, but which are not learned in the same way by working-class children which puts them at a severe disadvantage in terms of future life chances. Bourdieu argued that forms of educational assessment, which appear neutral, actually transform middle-class cultural competences into hierarchies of attainment, which then appear to be the outcomes of inequalities in natural ability. (See human capital; social capital.)

Curriculum

This refers either to the subject areas and content to be covered within a course or programme of learning provision, or to the programme of learning involved in a particular course or series of learning opportunities.

Curriculum 2000

Curriculum 2000 was launched in September 2000 and introduced a range of new and revised qualifications at advanced level. The qualifications were developed primarily for 16-19 year olds, following recommendations in the late 1990s that proposed greater breadth and flexibility in the post-16 curriculum. The reforms are intended to raise standards and widen participation in post-16 education. They are intended to encourage young people to study more subjects, provide an easier combination of academic and vocational study and encompass core subjects, Key Skills, tutorial and personal enrichment.

D

Deep learning

Deep learning is concerned with extracting principles and underlying meanings, to make sense of facts and feelings and to integrate them with previously acquired knowledge. (See surface learning.)

Democratic participation

Democratic participation means taking part in democratic activities such as voting, lobbying, attending meetings, joining political parties and/or pressure groups. The term refers to people's involvement in the government of society, either directly or through their elected representatives. Democratic participation can range from becoming, or voting for, members of parliament or local councillors, to becoming a school governor, management committee member, campaigner, taking part in a demonstration or writing to an elected representative or newspaper. (See citizenship education.)

Democratic renewal

Democratic renewal seeks to make democratic activity a way-of-life rather than simply a voting procedure. It involves re-engaging those who feel alienated (for whatever reason), powerless, or cynical about their ability to make a difference, and seeks to build democratic values into the working arrangements of all groups and organisations

Department for Education and Skills (DfES)

DfES is the Government body responsible for education and work based learning in England. It replaced the Department for Education and Employment in June 2001.

Development education

Refers to education programmes and approaches concerned to understand the nature and characteristics of societies (usually in the 'third' – or 'developing' – world, sometimes called 'the South') that are undergoing a late transition to capitalist economies and industrialised societies. The concern is generally about the effects of development on social groups who are poor. Increasingly development education seeks to raise the consciousness of those in more affluent societies about the inter-relationship between third world poverty and western economic and social policies, especially in the context of globalisation. (See Globalisation.)

Development trusts

Development trusts are usually community-based and concerned with the social, economic and environmental regeneration of a local area. They are community-owned and non-profit organisations.

Disability

Refers to a loss or lack of mental or physical functioning, which unlike illness is usually permanent (for example blindness or paralysis). People with disabilities are often viewed as being somehow 'dysfunctional' in societies in which prejudice and discrimination against minorities is not challenged or outlawed. (See Disability Discrimination Act; disabilist)

Disability Discrimination Act (DDA)

The Act has been in force since 1995. It now covers Disabled Employees (Part 2), Access to Goods and Services (Part 3) and Education (Part 4). Under DDA Part 4, universities, further education colleges and local education authorities providing adult and community education have a legal duty not to treat disabled learners less favourably for reasons related to their disability and also to provide reasonable adjustments for them. (See disability; disabilist.)

Disabilist

Actions or attitudes which discriminate against people with disabilities (for example in relation to education or employment) are sometimes called disablist in the same way as some forms of discrimination can be regarded as sexist (in relation to gender) or racist (in relation to ethnic minority groups). (See disability.)

Disaffected

Disaffected is a term that is usually applied to young people who are turned off or alienated from learning and wider society. The shortcoming of the term is that it can cast the person or group as the problem, rather than the school system or other aspects of society.

Discrimination

This term refers to treating someone unfairly and is most often used in relation to the less favourable treatment of minority and less powerful groups (especially in terms of race, ethnicity, gender, disability, sexuality, age etc) by more powerful groups within society. Discrimination is not simply a matter of unfair attitudes to minority groups, it implies actions that create and sustain inequalities of opportunity and outcomes.

Dissemination

The spreading or sharing of information so that others can learn from it. Examples of dissemination include the publication of findings, presenting information at conferences or seminars, or distributing videos.

Distance learning

Distance learning occurs when students are taught from a remote location for example by correspondence or ICT. It can also be a form of education which takes place outside 'normal' office or school hours, or where the pace of learning is significantly faster or slower than usual. Traditional distance education uses printed materials and correspondence between the learner and the tutor. Modern technology now allows the Internet to improve this by the use of computer conferencing, and other communication between learners and teachers, using voice, video, and course materials on the web.

Early Excellence Centres

These centres are part of a government initiative to offer models of good practice in early years education (the 0-5 years age group) in deprived areas. The centres provide high quality services for the children, families and communites they serve. They aim to provide children with a good start in life by combining early education, childcare and parent/carer provision, and multi-agency support.

Economically active

Economically active refers to people who are in paid employment or contributing to the economy e.g. volunteers. Economically active people may be unemployed but actively seeking work.

Education Action Zones (EAZ)

EAZ were set up in 1998 to develop new and imaginative approaches to raising standards in schools in disadvantaged urban and rural areas. The intention is for EAZs to become Excellence in Cities Action Zones (EiCAZs) or Excellence Clusters in 2005.

Education to Employment (E2E)

The E2E programme, introduced in England in 2003, replaced Life Skills, Preparatory Training and NVQ Learning at Level 1. It is targeted at young people who are not ready or able to enter Modern Apprenticeships, further education or employment.

The programme helps participants to prepare for progression to employment, employment with training, Modern Apprenticeships and further education The participation target for the first year was 47,000 young people over the age of 16. (See Modern Apprenticeships.)

E-learning

E-learning is the delivery of learning and training activities through the use of electronic media, including the Internet, intranet, extranet, CD-ROM, video tape, interactive television, phones. E-learning may also include the use of e-technology to support traditional methods of learning, for example using electronic whiteboards or video conferencing.

E-learning can be customised to the need of the individual and has the flexibility to allow studying at a pace, time and location that best suits the learner, thereby giving the potential to provide widespread access to training and education.

Emancipatory learning

Emancipatory learning aims to develop understanding and knowledge about the nature and root causes of unsatisfactory life circumstances in order to develop real strategies for change. The learning relates to social justice and greater equality through working with people (usually the least powerful and socially excluded) to gain more autonomy, independence and more control over their lives. This type of learning is relevant today due to increasing inequalities within and between countries. While education cannot change economic and class systems it can play a part in raising awareness and assisting people in their struggles against discrimination, exploitation, inequalities and social injustices. It can make a difference to people's lives when heightened awareness connects with increased understanding and joint action to bring about changes. Emancipatory learning is particularly relevant in community development and community based learning.

Embedded basic skills

Embedded basic skills is the teaching of numeracy and literacy skills within the context of another subject area that initially attracts the learner to learning provision, such as aromatherapy, ICT skills or local history. Integrating basic skills into other subjects has been found more relevant and interesting to some groups of learners than non-embedded basic skills learning programmes.

Employer Training Pilots

Employer Training Pilots were introduced in 2002 in six areas (now to be extended to 18) to encourage companies, especially small and medium-sized enterprises (SMEs) to train low-skilled staff and help them achieve a qualification. The incentive for firms is that the Government provides funding to subsidise the cost of sending employees on training courses. In the first year of operation, 300 employers, the majority of them SMEs, and 1300 employees were involved in the pilots. Many of the workers involved were members of groups that are usually excluded from employer-supported training.

English Local Labour Force Survey (ELLFS)

ELLFS is a partnership project between the Department of Education and Skills (DfES), the Office for National Statistics (ONS) and the Department for Work and Pensions (DWP), to provide statistics on adult participation at a local level. The survey which began in 2001, uses a sample size of 60,000 adults, with a cohort of 12,000 added each quarter. Each cohort is interviewed quarterly 5 times – securing a sample size large enough to produce statistically robust data for each local and learning skills council (LLSC) and each Local Education Authority area. ELLFS gives a participation rate for each of the 47 LLSCs, enabling realistic targets to be set for each area. In addition, ELLFS can track participation nationally among population groups who are priorities for widening participation. The survey reports annually each October.

Equal opportunities
The term is usually used in relation to policies and practices within organisations to ensure that they operate on the assumption that agreed and fair procedures are necessary to safeguard the interests of minority and less powerful groups when it comes to distributing rewards and opportunities. In an educational context, the commitment to equality of opportunity implies that all individuals, regardless of class, race, gender, sexuality, age etc, should have the same opportunities to learn and develop their potential. Inequalities of outcome are deemed legitimate if they reflect differences in merit and ability rather than differences based on unfavourable treatment or historic discrimination.

ESOL stands for **E**nglish courses or programmes for **S**peakers of **O**ther **L**anguages.

Ethnicity, ethnic group, ethnic minority
Ethnicity defines people who consider themselves, or who are considered by others, to share common cultural characteristics such as identity, religion, language, politics or traditions. The individuals concerned are not necessarily identifiable in terms of racial origins or attributes (for example Jews) and their sense of collective identity may well change in relation to the shift of populations (for example Indians in Britain are considered to constitute a single ethnic group whilst the same individuals in India would be identified as members of quite different groupings, related to e.g. caste or language). The basis of ethnicity lies in social and cultural descriptions and not in biological or physical characteristics. Minority ethnic group refers to those groups which are in a numerical minority in a given society.

Ethnocentrism
Ethnocentrism is the belief in the superiority of one's own cultural group or society and is often associated with a dislike or misunderstanding of other such groups. In an educational context, the term refers to the teaching of a subject or design of course materials biased towards the beliefs, values and culture of a dominant group or nation.

European Credit Transfer System (ECTS)

This is also known as 'the Bologna Process'. It is a system designed to enable students to receive credits for their work at one university which will be recognised by other universities, either in the same or another European country.

European Social Fund (ESF)

ESF is a funding source that aims to promote development in regional economies that are lagging behind the rest of Europe. The fund focuses on providing people with work and social skills to improve their self-confidence and adaptability in the labour market. The aim is to promote equal access to work by men and women, the disabled and disadvantaged groups at risk of social exclusion. The ESF is an important source of funding for activities to develop education, employment and training schemes. The ESF is revenue funding and can often provide match funding to other types of government funding.

Evaluation

An evaluation is an activity involving monitoring and assessing the effectiveness of any actions or procedures undertaken to achieve the planned aims and objectives of a project, course programme or organisation. The results of evaluations can help in decision-making and planning future actions.

Evaluations can use a range of quantitative and qualitative indicators to measure progress. They can be carried out by those involved in the project (self evaluation), or an independent person or agency (external evaluation). Often, the monitoring and review process informs evaluation. (See learner evaluation.)

Exit strategy

This is action planned to manage the completion of a project or scheme and, where possible, to ensure its longer term survival at the end of its projected timescale. The strategy should identify the arrangements to be put in place for winding up, letting go, or moving on from projects when funding comes to an end, in ways that do not leave participants feeling abandoned without any support. If a project does not have a natural end, funders often want some assurance that it is sustainable or that someone else will be prepared to take over the responsibility for providing resources and support.

Experiential learning

Experiential learning is derived from everyday experience in the workplace, in the home, in the community or, informally, in education settings. There is increasing recognition that such learning can be valuable and can broaden, underpin and extend learning, which is formally conducted and assessed. (See assessment or accreditation of prior (experiential) learning.)

F

Family learning
Family learning encompasses a wide range of formal and informal learning activities that set out to develop skills in, and understanding of, family roles, relationships and responsibilities. 'Families' are understood to include not just parents, grandparents and children who are biologically related, but also other relatives and individuals who may be involved in parenting and caring roles, including, for example, childminders and foster parents. While some family learning involves adults and children learning together through shared activities and experiences, it may also involve learning in separate age groups which can then be applied in family situations.

Feasibility study
Funders may want evidence that a project is feasible before investing large sums of money in it. A feasibility study should make clear the conditions under which a project is workable. It might involve looking at the experience of similar enterprises; thinking through practical problems; making projections about level of use and the resources required, considering how income will be future generated and sustained, and specifying the management and organisational requirements.

Financial literacy
Financial literacy is a skill involving the responsible use of money and making informed financial decisions regarding the use and management of money. The increase in the number of individuals and households in debt highlights the importance of developing financial literacy programmes to equip people with the skills to help them avoid financial problems. (The Adult Financial Capability Framework refers to financial capability instead of financial literacy.)

First-rung provision
This is learning provision, often of an informal nature, provided on behalf of, or in response to the requirements or interests of, people returning to organised learning for the first time since leaving school.

First Steps
First Steps provision is designed to enable learners to progress over time, in a vertical direction, on to accredited programmes at level 2. It is currently funded through further education and adult community learning funding streams. In the future Local Learning and Skills Councils will contract with adult education organ-

isations, the voluntary sector or further education to provide a specific volume of this provision based on what they consider they need, for example to increase their chances of meeting targets for level 2 qualifications, and what they can afford to purchase.

Focus groups
The convening of small groups, for research or consultation purposes, to consider and discuss issues of interest to them.

Formal learning
Formal learning generally refers to a structured learning programme for which there is an established curriculum and externally determined standards. Formal learning can be provided by an education or training centre or institution, an employing organisation, a professional body or a voluntary organisation. The learning is structured and usually leads to some form of certification. (See informal learning; non-formal learning.)

Formative evaluation
In the context of a learning programme, formative evaluation refers to evaluation that takes place throughout a project or programme with the aim of assisting and improving a learner's progress. It can also apply to the development and review process of a project or activity. The evaluation strategy is usually established at the outset, with evaluation activities taking place throughout the duration of the project. This provides an opportunity to modify or make changes to the project during its lifetime. (See Summative evaluation.)

Formula funding
This involves the application of funding arrangements, based on specific central criteria, to state-funded education provision.

Forums
Forums are assemblies of people who come together either as individuals, or to represent others, to discuss or make decisions about issues they have in common. (See learners' forum.)

Foundation degrees
Foundation degrees, launched in 2001, are two-year, vocational qualifications, planned in association with employers, and delivered mainly in further education colleges or higher education institutions. They can be full or part time, and may lead to a final year at a designated local university as a 'top-up' to an honours degree.

Funding methodology
In a post- 16 context, a funding methodology is determined by a funding agency such as the Learning and Skills Council or HEFCE. It identifies the criteria used to determine how public money is provided for education and training. It can calculate the income to be gained from particular arrangements, as well as offer incentives/disincentives which make certain types of programmes, and possibly learners, 'more attractive' in financial terms, thus influencing the way the curriculum and institutional practices develop.

Further education (FE)
In general the term 'further education' embraces the whole post-secondary education sector excluding higher education. This includes academic, vocational and general education for young people and adults. More specifically the term refers to further education colleges and the learning programmes they provide.

G

Gatekeepers
Gatekeepers are individuals who are in close contact with particular groups and who, by virtue of this relationship and their authority over the groups in question, are able to exercise some control over access to them by other people. Examples include employers, managers (for example, of voluntary groups), health visitors, religious leaders and wardens (for example, of day centres, bail hostels and residential homes). Gatekeepers can be useful for facilitating access to individuals considered to be 'hard to reach' and directing people to local learning facilities, as a result of the trust they have built up with them. Gatekeepers can also prevent other agencies from making contact with groups through territorial concerns or over-protectiveness.

General National Vocational Qualification (GNVQ)
GNVQs offer students over the age of 16 in England, Wales and Northern Ireland an alternative to traditional GCE A Level and GCSEs. GNVQs provide a broad base of vocationally relevant knowledge and skills in preparation either for entry into work or for progression into higher education. There are three GNVQ Levels:

- foundation – equivalent to four GCSEs at grades D-G, normally taken after one year's full time study
- intermediate – equivalent to four GCSEs at grades A-C, normally taken after one year's full time study.

- advanced – vocational A levels equivalent to two GCE A levels, normally taken after two years full time study

Students may take a full GNVQ along with other qualifications such as a GCE A levels, AS courses or additional GNVQ or NVQ units.

All GNVQs include three compulsory key skill units – Communication, Application of Number, and Information Technology.

For 14 to 16 year olds, there is a Part One GNVQ which is equivalent to half a full GNVQ.

Generic skills

Generic skills are those skills which are thought to be fundamental to undertaking specific activities, and which are essential to performing well in the specified activity. (See transferable skills.)

Globalisation

Globalisation refers to the emergence of a global economic and cultural system brought about by a number of different factors, such as the existence of a world satellite information system, the development of global patterns of production and trade linked to free market economics, the development of global patterns of consumption and consumerism, the decline in the sovereignty of the nation state, the recognition of a world-wide ecological crisis and the increasingly complex interdependency (and mutual antagonism) of nations around issues of poverty, health and well being and national security.

The impact of globalisation is important in relation to education policy and practice for three main reasons: (i) The starting point of the government's knowledge and skills agenda is to secure a labour force that can function and compete in the global market place. (ii) The globalisation of knowledge production and cultural production creates a much larger arena in which British knowledge and culture seek to have influence. (iii) Social inequalities (both globally and locally) are exacerbated by globalisation. Learners need to understand the impact of global processes on their lives in order to inform their political response.

Government Offices (GOs)

The local GOs are government outposts in the nine English regions, which help to ensure that government initiatives are working at a local level. They also reflect the needs of the regions back to central government.

GRUNDTVIG

GRUNDVIG is a source of European funding under the Socrates programme which aims to strengthen the European dimension in adult education and lifelong learning. It targets adult learners, teachers and trainers in both formal and non-formal education across Europe in a range of projects and initiatives, and reflects a commitment at national and European level to ensure that learning opportunities continue throughout life. (See Socrates.)

The term takes its origin from a Danish clergyman and writer Nikolai Grundtvig (1783-1872) who is regarded as the founder of the Nordic tradition of lifelong learning.

H

Hard outcome
A hard outcome is a measurable end-result of a service or activity such as a qualification, a completed training course or an employment opportunity. (See soft outcome.)

Hard-to-reach
This term is often used to describe groups or communities who experience economic disadvantage and social exclusion for reasons such as age, race, disability or poverty. In many cases these groups have had poor educational experiences of school and have characteristically left the education system early with few qualifications. This has resulted in their being 'turned off' education and reluctant to return to learning at a later stage. Hard-to-reach learners may also include those who have had some education but have been unable to put their learning to use. As a result they have become disillusioned by the education system.

The term has been criticised for placing a negative emphasis on groups or individuals rather than on the failure of learning providers to appeal and suit those individuals or groups.

Health Action Zones (HAZs)
HAZs consist of partnerships between the NHS, local authorities, community and voluntary groups and the business sector. They have been set up to develop locally agreed strategies and programmes to help improve the health of local people in deprived areas over a seven-year period, with funding continuing to 2006.

HAZs deal with a wide range of issues that affect health including housing, employment and education. (See Action Zones.)

Health literacy
In 1998 the World Health Organisation defined health literacy as:

"The cognitive and social skills which determine the motivation and ability of individuals to gain access to, understand and use information in ways which promote and mange good health."

Three levels of health literacy have been distinguished that reflect increasing degrees of autonomy and empowerment:

- functional health literacy assumes sufficient basic skills in reading and writing to be able to understand a simple health message and the ability to comply with expert-prescribed actions to maintain health or remedy the problem.
- interactive health literacy involves more advanced cognitive and literacy skills which, together with social skills, can be used to manage health problems in partnership with health professionals.
- critical health literacy describes more advanced skills, which can be used to analyse information critically, and to use this information to increase awareness of one's situation and thereby exert greater control over life events.

The Higher Education Funding Council for England (HEFCE)
This is a Government body, established in 1992, responsible for funding higher education institutions and Higher Education in other institutions. HEFCE is also responsible for quality assurance, and for ensuring that higher education institutions have strategies, for example in widening participation. There is an equivalent body in Wales, the Higher Education Funding Council for Wales (HEFCW).

Higher education (HE)
HE can be defined as study at university level. HE courses are at undergraduate level (leading typically to BA or BSC degrees) or at postgraduate level (MA, MSc or PhD). There is also a range of sub-degree courses. HE courses can be full or part time, and studied on a university or college campus, or by distance learning, as with the Open University. (See further education)

Higher Education Institution (HEI)
A higher education institution is typically a university or similar institution where degree-level, sub-degree level and postgraduate study can be undertaken.

Higher National Certificate (HNC)
An HNC is a vocational qualification, of higher value than the NVQ but lower value than the HND.

Higher National Diploma (HND)

This is a vocational qualification equivalent to a Foundation degree or two years study on a conventional degree programme.

Homophobia

This is a term that originally referred to people's psychological fear of homosexuality and lesbianism. The term is now more widely used to mean prejudiced and hostile attitudes, and treatment of lesbian and homosexual people.

Human capital

Human capital refers to the knowledge and skills that enable people to function in economic and social life. In current usage the emphasis is usually on the former, with the term generally understood to refer to the skills and attributes that individuals can contribute to the economy. It is often observed that post-compulsory educational policy is more concerned with the development of human capital than with the development of social or cultural capital. (See cultural capital; social capital.)

In-kind funding

This relates to non-financial contributions to a project, such as offering access to facilities or professional expertise.

Independent learning

This is a method of study in which individual learners work on their own, whether on a learning programme devised by educational providers or in pursuit of their own interests. The term is often used in association with open learning.

Indices of Deprivation

These are government-defined measures of deprivation for every ward and local authority in England. They combine a number of indicators (income, employment, health deprivation and disability, education, skills and training, housing and geographical access to services), which jointly add up to a single deprivation score for each area.

Individual Learner Record (ILR)

The ILR is used in the further education sector (and now also in the adult and community learning sectors funded by the Learning and Skills Council (LSC)), to keep track of the studying and training undertaken by learners. The data gathered from ILRs provides information about the progress of students to assist the LSC in managing and evaluating existing programmes.

Individual Learning Plan (ILP)

An ILP is an agreement between a student and an education provider or a company that is supporting work-based training. It sets out the aims and objectives of learning or training programmes and a series of interim goals that all sides agree are reasonable and attainable.

Informal learning

There is no consensus on the meaning of this term. It is often used to refer to the intentional learning that people undertake independently (for example through reading, attending a talk). It is also often defined as the unintentional incidental learning that results from daily activities related to family, work or leisure.

Information, Advice and Guidance (IAG)

In an adult learning context, this refers to a process of informing, advising and guiding individuals or groups on entry to, during or on exit from a learning activity. Since 2001 provision of IAG on learning has been the responsibility of the Learning and Skills Council.

There are 67 local IAG partnerships in place across England. These bring together local IAG providers to produce significant improvements in the quality and coverage of local services. Publicly funded providers are required to comply with the matrix standard for IAG services, but beyond this there is no imposed uniform model.

Information and Communications Technology (ICT)

ICT is the electronic storage, processing and presentation of information through a number of media. Within education, the technologies generally focus around delivering information to support learning processes. Basic computer and key-board skills are now necessary for large numbers of jobs and are seen as essential skills alongside language, literacy and numeracy. (See Basic Skills)

Infrastructure

When used in relation to organisations, enterprises or projects, infrastructure refers to the basic structural elements of the enterprise. For an organisation this would include a building or meeting place, finance and staffing, management and operating systems.

Institutional racism

Institutional racism is the idea that racial discrimination against some groups in society can result from the majority simply going along unthinkingly with existing organisational arrangements, membership, institutional rules or social norms. The cumulative affect of organisational attitudes and practices which perpetuate ignorance, prejudice or discrimination, however unthinking, leads to a culture of institutional racism.

Overt prejudice, hostility and discrimination need not be demonstrated for institutionalised racism to be present, although in practice both forms usually go hand-in-hand.

Interactive methods of teaching and learning

These are techniques which encourage the active interaction between learners and tutors, and are as distinct from the passive receiving of information.

Intermediate Labour Market

This involves schemes that combine training and waged work experience. They aim to provide stepping-stones into work for people with experience of long-term unemployment. The schemes are often subsidised or supported by public sector or voluntary sources of finance.

Investors in People (IiP)

IiP is the national standard for good practice in the training and development of employees to achieve their own and workplace goals. It is aimed at boosting efficiency, productivity and staff motivation by creating a climate of 'continuous improvement'. Companies are assessed annually or once every three years.

J

Joined-up (practice, working)

This means working strategically, in partnership with other appropriate bodies, in accordance with appropriate plans and initiatives. It also means sharing information on specific areas of social and economic policy. The idea is that different agencies or departments should plan and work together to achieve more successful implementation of policy. This term is used with particular reference to national or local government departments.

K

Key Skills
Key skills are a range of essential skills such as communication, literacy, number skills and ICT which the government believes are necessary to underpin success in education, training and employment. It is argued that key skills are essential if individuals are to compete effectively in the labour markets of the 21st century.

Key skills qualifications
These were introduced in September 2000 across England, Wales and Northern Ireland They are available at levels 1 to 4 and are normally offered as part of a wider programme (e.g. alongside an AS/A level or as part of an apprenticeship). Students can obtain Key Skills awards in Communication, Application of Number and Information Technology.

Kolb's learning cycle
This is a learning model developed by David Kolb that presents a way of structuring a session or a whole course using a learning cycle. The stages of the cycle are; concrete experience, observations and reflection, formation of abstract concepts and generalisations and testing implications of concepts in new situations.

L

Labour Force Survey
This is a national survey of individuals, currently published quarterly, which asks questions about their involvement in education, training and the labour market.

Learndirect
Learndirect is a network of online learning and information services, which were introduced across England, Wales and Northern Ireland in October 2000. The network provides information about learning opportunities. It links up with the 'University For Industry' which works with over 600 partners including a broad range of public and private providers to deliver mainly online courses and information through a network of learning centres. Alternatively, individuals can study at home or work if they have access to the internet. (See University for Industry.)

Learner-centred learning/provision
Learner-centred provision is education or training which puts the emphasis on learning and the needs of the learner rather than on instruction and institutional or academic interests.

Learner Satisfaction Survey
The Learner Satisfaction Survey has been commissioned by the Learning and Skills Council (LSC) to measure the degree of satisfaction amongst learners in the post-16 education and training sector across England. The aim of the survey is to establish national criteria that will, over time, reveal longer-term trends and highlight any necessary improvements. The findings will help the LSC shape its future policies and ensure that its services meet the needs of learners.

The first survey was published in November 2002. It covers further education students, work-based learning trainees and adult learners in adult and community learning.

Learning and Skills Council, (LSC) and Local Learning and Skills Councils, (LLSC)
The Learning and Skills Council (LSC), established in 2001, is responsible for all post-16 education in England other than the university sector, including the planning and funding of further education colleges, school sixth forms, work-based training for young people, workforce development, adult and community learning, information and guidance for adults, and education links. It operates through a national office and 47 Local Learning and Skills Councils (LLSC).

Learning and Training at Work (LTW)
LTW is a regular statistical survey conducted by the Office for National Statistics. It presents figures on key indicators of employers' commitment to training. This includes the management and delivery of training and the levels of provision of both off-the-job and on-the-job training. The LTW also records employers' awareness of, and involvement with, various training initiatives.

Learning centres
Learning centres provide access to learning in places accessible to the learner, such as at work or in a local community centre. The centres are also known as satellite centres (centres in local community areas which are part of a main centre such as a further education college). The centres tend to involve a significant investment in IT.

Learning champions/Learning ambassadors
These are people who act as advocates for learning in their own social or working communities. They are usually people who have themselves recently successfully

undertaken learning, often overcoming personal and practical barriers in order to do so. Learning champions are often more credible to their peers than profess-ionals. There are training schemes for learning champions.

Learning difficulties/learning disabilities

The term learning difficulties tends to be used in education while the term learning disabilities is used more in health and social services settings. However, they both mean the same thing. The terms cover people who find some activities that involve thinking and understanding difficult and who need additional help and support with their everyday lives. People with learning difficulties have problems under-standing, learning and remembering new things, and in generalising any learning to new situations. This can lead to difficulties with a number of social tasks, for example communication, self-care, awareness of health and safety. Some people with learning difficulties may also have an additional impairment such as a sensory impairment or a physical disability.

Learning environment

This is the domain where learning occurs for example a formal education institution, the work place, a community setting, a voluntary organisation or the home.

Learning journey/learning pathway

This is the route an individual learner takes as they engage in different learning activities.

Learning Levels

In a learning context, levels are used to define specific levels of achievement which are used for educational benchmarking and national targets. They are generally linked to specific qualifications (although not everyone agrees with these equiva-lences). For example:

- Level 1 is defined as below GCSE level or the equivalent of a D-G grade GCSE
- Level 2 is defined as 5 GCSEs at grade A* – C; an NVQ 2 or a GNVQ
- Level 3 is defined as 2 good A levels or their vocational equivalent
- Level 4 is a degree or equivalent

Learning Management System (LMS)

LMS is an Internet-based software in educational institutions that deploys, man-ages, tracks and reports on interaction between learners, their programme of study and their tutors. Learning management systems perform student registration, track learner progress, record test scores, and indicate course completions. The system provides information for managers to pass to funding agencies and for tutors to keep up with student performance.

Learning outcome

A learning outcome is an effect that results on from a learning episode. Broadly speaking it means what a learner has acquired at the end of a given learning period. Outcomes for learners can include qualifications and wider benefits, including soft outcomes, such as an increase in self-esteem and confidence. As well as outcomes for the particular learner there can be wider outcomes such as the impact or effect on other people, the local community and the environment.

Outcomes are often contrasted with outputs. For instance, six people completing a training course is an output of the work, whereas a successful course mark would be an outcome.

Learning partnerships/Lifelong Learning Partnerships/ Local Learning Partnerships (LLPs)

These LLPs are local partnerships between learning providers and other relevant agencies set up shortly before the Learning and Skills Act 2000 to bring greater co-ordination and coherence into local educational planning. They are designed to help the Local Learning and Skills Councils in the process of identifying what provision is offered in their area, what gaps exist and what learners and potential learners want and need.

Learning society

A learning society is a term that became commonly used in the 1990s. It is seen by government as a desirable social as well as an economic goal. It is a society in which people are encouraged to learn throughout their lives, and where opportunities to participate in education and training are available to all.

Lifelong learning

This is a term for which there is no universally accepted definition but which implies a learning process that continues throughout life according to the needs of people at different stages of their life-cycle/lifespan. Most western societies now subscribe to the principle of lifelong learning, however few have yet to put in place the necessary structures and resources that would make this possible. In England, for example, the term is now infrequently used in policy documents as greatest priority is given to those in the 14–19 cohorts. The term 'lifelong learning' is often used synonymously with longer-established terms, such as adult education and adult and continuing education. (See life-wide learning.)

Life skills

The term refers to those psychosocial and interpersonal skills which help individuals to make informed decisions, communicate effectively, and develop coping and self-management skills that are necessary to lead a healthy and productive life.

Life-wide Learning

Life-wide learning is a term often used in conjunction with lifelong learning to take account of the spread of learning across a person's daily life. The idea being that learning occurs wherever you are.

Local Education Authorities (LEAs)

LEAs have the day-to-day responsibility for providing and maintaining primary and secondary education in their local areas. LEAs also secure or provide adult education. There are 150 LEAs in England and 25 in Wales. Many LEAs organise a range of both accredited and non-accredited classes and courses for adults, through their own adult and community learning services or in conjunction with partners commissioned to provide learning on their behalf. LEAs also work with Local Learning and Skills Councils and other partnerships to ensure that there is a range of local post-16 education programmes in their areas to meet the skills and training needs of the area.

Local Learning and Skills Councils (LLSC) – see Learning and Skills Council.

Local Strategic Partnerships (LSPs)

LSPs are partnerships made up of organisations and local representatives, led by local authorities and concerned with strategies to deliver better local services in the interest of neighbourhood renewal. They involve representatives from public, private, business, community and voluntary sectors. LSPs are increasingly the mechanism through which community strategies are developed and regeneration and development money is delivered. They are required to involve local people in shaping the future of their neighbourhood and how services are provided.

M

Managed Learning Environment (MLE)

This is a structured technology based environment that manages, or contributes to the management, of information and systems within an educational institution. A virtual learning environment can be subsumed within the infrastructure of an MLE to enhance teaching and learning.

Management Information System (MIS)

MIS is the computerised system used in formal education institutions to store information on enrolments and learners' programmes of study, retention, progress and achievements. (See Learning Management System.)

Match funding

Match funding refers to the money or in-kind resources (e.g. people or facilities) required by a funding body (e.g. European Social Fund) as a condition for receiving financial support for projects or other initiatives.

Mentors

Mentors are people who are trained to support and encourage others to adapt to a new working (or learning) environment and achieve their goals. Mentors usually share characteristics and experiences in common with those they mentor. This gives them the knowledge, understanding and empathy they need to act effectively. Acting as a guide, supporter and assessor, the mentor can considerably add to the value of the learning experience. Using existing students as mentors has been found to be an effective way of helping non-traditional students into further or higher education programmes.

Modern Apprenticeships (MAs)

MAs are work-based programmes which offer young people aged over 16 the opportunity to train while in a paid job and to gain a nationally recognised qualification based on vocational skills. They also provide the opportunity to train in key skills such as information technology, team working and effective communication. They are available in over 80 different sectors of industry and commerce.

MAs usually last up to three years and offer work-based training at two levels. The Foundation Modern Apprenticeship (formerly called a National Traineeship) leads to a National Vocational Qualification (NVQ) level 2 and the Advanced Modern Apprenticeship leads to a higher NVQ. Apprentices progress from a Foundation programme to the Advanced level and then, if they wish, go on to pursue further qualifications in higher education.

In 2003 it was announced that the age cap on MAs would be removed so that they would be available to adults aged 25+.

Module

This is a separate and coherent block of learning that is usually part of a programme of study where the curriculum is divided into a number of similar sized segments. Modular programmes are divided into self-contained units or modules from which students can select units and acquire points for successful completion of each. These points can build up to a qualification. The emphasis is on flexibility and maximising student choice.

Monitoring

Monitoring is the process of checking against plans, milestones, goals and targets to ensure that a learning project or programme, or learners themselves, are progressing towards identified outcomes. Monitoring can be vital when the funding of learning is related to specific outputs.

N

National Adult Learning Survey (NALS)

This is a survey commissioned by the Department for Education and Skills (DfES) to monitor the effectiveness of its adult learning policies, and progress in meeting the National Learning Targets for adult participation.

A baseline study, covering a representative sample of 5,500 adults, was undertaken in 1997, followed by repeat surveys in 2000 and 2001. The samples for NALS 1997 and 2000 were selected from all adults aged 16-69 (in England and Wales), with the age cap lifted in 2001.

Given the sample size, the NALS results cannot yet be disaggregated by LSC area or by skills and employment sectors.

National Learning Targets

These are set to achieve improvements and increase participation and achievement in some areas of learning. Current targets include improvements in basic skills among both children and adults, increases in the number of adults achieving a level two qualification, and a target to increase the number of people aged 18-30 entering higher education.

National Open College Network (NOCN)

The NOCN is the UK's foremost provider of accreditation services for adult learners. NOCN is a recognised national qualification awarding body and is the central organisation for 28 Open College Networks (OCNs) based across the UK. NOCN provides national qualifications and programmes in a wide range of subject areas and offers a local accreditation service through the OCNs that provides recognition of achievement through the award of credit.

NOCN also works in partnership with organisations to develop learning strategies that will enable people to participate and succeed. The fully integrated service of accreditation and qualifications helps to secure provision relevant to learners and employers, with robust standards, achievable goals and progression oppor-tunities for all.

National Qualifications Framework

The national qualifications framework is a way of organising and assuring quality in qualifications in England, Wales and Northern Ireland. It embraces general and vocational qualifications that are underpinned by key skills. It also aims to promote lifelong learning by helping people to understand clear routes of progression, as well as to avoid unnecessary duplication and overlapping of qualifications. The framework provides a coherent range of qualifications that meet the need of students, employers and higher education. It shows how qualifications relate to each other. There are three main kinds of qualification included in the framework:

* **General qualifications**, such as GCSEs and A levels, which are about a particular subject, like history, maths or English.
* **Vocationally-related qualifications**, such as vocational A levels (Advanced GNVQs), which give a broad introduction to a particular sector of the economy, for example engineering or the media.
* **Occupational qualifications**, such as NVQs (National Vocational Qualifications), test the skills and knowledge needed to do a specific job.

Qualifications in the national framework range from entry-level awards to profess-ional qualifications at level 5. The higher the level of a qualification, the greater the depth and breadth of knowledge, skills and understanding are required to receive it. Entry-level awards act as stepping stones to the lower levels of the framework.

National Training Organisations (NTOs)

NTOs are independent, employer-led sector organisations throughout the whole of Great Britain, which work strategically with their sectors and with Government across education and training. NTOs aim to assist the Government to extend and improve its dialogue with employers to ensure that the needs of business are taken fully into account in developing policy. NTOs are concerned with: identifying skill shortages and the training needs of the whole of their sector influencing education and careers guidance provision; developing occupational standards and NVQs and advising on the national qualifications structure; influencing and advising on train-ing arrangements and training solutions; effective communications and networking with their employer base and key partners to implement strategies.

NTOs have existed since 1998 but most went out of business in 2004. Industry sectors will then move into a smaller number of 'sector skills councils'. (See Sector Skills Development Agencies; Sector Skills Councils)

National Vocational Qualifications (NVQs)

These are work-specific vocational qualifications and competence-based qualifications that reflect the skills and knowledge needed to do a job effectively. The qualifications are aimed at people in, or aiming to, enter the labour market. The qualifications represent national standards recognised by employers throughout the country (the equivalent in Scotland are called Scottish Vocational Qualifications (SVQs)). (See national qualifications framework)

Needs analysis

This is a method for identifying what people's learning needs are in order that solutions and remedies can be sought. A needs analysis brings together evidence, both formal and informal, which has been collected form specific groups and communities.

Neighbourhood Renewal

The term neighbourhood renewal was first used in 1998 by the government's Social Exclusion Unit in its report '*Bringing Britain Back Together: A National Strategy for Neighbourhood Renewal*' to address the problems it had identified in Britain's most deprived areas. These included poverty, long-term unemployment, poor housing stock, run down neighbourhoods and derelict environments, significant exposure to crime, failing local services and widespread disengagement from civil society and formal participation processes.

In January 2001 the government launched a twenty year Neighbourhood Renewal Action Plan concerned to close the gap between the richest and poorest areas of the country.

Neighbourhood Renewal Fund (NRF)

The Neighbourhood Renewal Fund aims to narrow the gap between deprived areas and the rest of England by providing funds to enable the 88 most deprived authorities, in collaboration with their Local Strategic Partnership (LSP), to improve public services. As part of the Spending Review 2002, the Government announced that an additional £975m will be made available for the NRF in 2004-05 and 2005-06 as part of its strategy to further benefit England's poorest neighbourhoods.

Neighbourhood Renewal Unit

This is a unit based in the Office of the Deputy Prime Minister, which is responsible for developing and delivering the government's national strategy for neighbourhood renewal.

Neighbourhood Support Fund
The Neighbourhood Support Fund is targeted at young people between the ages of 13 and 19. Its aims are to develop and enhance young people's confidence and skills, so that they are able to overcome barriers to both learning and work. The funds are split between several managing agents, who are collectively responsible for around 650 community-based projects in 40 of the most deprived local authorities in England today.

Networks
Networks are informal, loose collections of organisations or individuals who share common interests, goals and concerns. Networks might be issue-based, field- or sector-based. The purpose of networks, or being part of one, is usually to promote, disseminate and acquire information to keep each other up-to-date with what is going on, identify opportunities for partnership working or opportunities to influence policy. Networks may develop into more formal, focused structures with specific and restricted membership, like coalitions.

New Deal
The New Deal programme was introduced for unemployed young people in 1997 and has since been rolled out with other priority groups. The scheme aims to improve people's employability through offering individualised support and a set menu of options, all including work experience and training. There are now six main programmes which vary according to target group, aims and objectives, eligibility rules, and the type of support offered.
The *New Deal for Young People* (NDYP) is targeted on individuals aged 18 to 24 who have been unemployed for at least six months. It is compulsory, and includes a gateway period of advice and support followed by one of four options (subsidised employment, full-time education and training, voluntary work, environmental work).

New Deal for Long-term Unemployed (NDLTU)
NDLTU is targeted on individuals aged 25 plus who have been unemployed for 12, 18 or 24 months (depending on area). Participants receive advice and support from Personal Advisers and there are two main options (subsidised employment and education/ training).

New Deal for Lone Parents (NDLP)
NDLP is voluntary and consists of an initial interview with a Personal Adviser, case loading, job search and in-work support. The target group is lone mothers on Income Support for six months or more and with a youngest child aged five years and three months or over.

New Deal for Partners of Unemployed People (NDPU)

NDPU is aimed at partners of unemployed jobseekers. It is voluntary and offers two options. Those without children aged 18 to 24 can participate in the NDYP. Those aged 18 to 24 with children, and those aged 25 plus, can have access to advice and guidance from a Personal Adviser.

New Deal for Disabled People (NDDP)

NDDP is voluntary and offers access to advice and information through a Personal Adviser. It is also intended to raise awareness of the employment needs of people with disabilities among employers and service providers.

New Deal for People Aged 50 and Above (ND50+)

ND50+ is another voluntary programme targeted at those aged 50 and over who have been receiving incapacity benefits or Jobseeker's Allowance/Income Support (JSA/IS) for at least six months. It offers access to a Personal Adviser and those finding work can receive an employment credit for up to one year.

New Deal for Communities (NDC)

NDC is a long-term (10-year) programme in the Government's strategy to tackle multiple deprivation in the most deprived neighbourhoods in the country, giving some of the poorest communities the resources to tackle their problems in an intensive and co-ordinated way through partnerships with key agencies. All NDC partnerships are tackling five key themes: poor job prospects; high levels of crime; educational under-achievement; poor health; and problems with housing and the physical environment.

Since 1998, approximately £2bn has been committed to 39 partnerships. An extensive system of support and advice is available to each partnership, including access to Neighbourhood Renewal Advisers and regional networks to build capacity in NDC neighbourhoods. The keys to change have been identified as improving local services, increasing community capacity and adopting an evidence-based approach to deliver change.

New Opportunities Fund (NOF)

The fund was created in 1998 and has merged with the Community Fund to become The Big Lottery Fund. The New Opportunities Fund distributes National Lottery funds for health, education and environment initiatives throughout the UK. As well as the Community Access to Lifelong Learning programme, the fund is currently funding healthy living centres, out-of-school hours childcare, out-of-school hours learning activities, ICT training for teachers, school librarians and librarians, and the digitisation of learning materials. The grants are aimed particularly at those in society who are most disadvantaged.

Non-accredited learning/provision
This is learning/provision which does not lead to an external certificate, award or qualification.

Non-formal learning
There is no consensus on the meaning of this term. It is often used to refer to learning that is initiated and controlled by learners themselves. This may be structured and may involve a teacher or instructor but it will not necessarily conform to an externally controlled curriculum or imposed standards (See formal learning; informal learning)

Non-Government Organisation (NGO)
An NGO is an independent organisation which often enjoys charitable status and is usually concerned with activities to address and change social, political and environmental conditions. NGOs are typically value-based organisations with a strong vision of social justice and progressive social change which depend, in whole or in part, on charitable donations and voluntary service, for example Oxfam and Friends of the Earth.

Non-participants
Non-participants is a term frequently used by professionals to refer to people who do not participate in organised learning provision after leaving school. Some people contest the term, as it is often used negatively and can imply criticism or blame. It also ignores the other forms of learning in which people engage.

Non-Schedule 2
In the 1992 Further and Higher Education Act, non-accredited leisure courses were categorised as non-Schedule 2 and responsibility for their provision was given to local education authorities (LEAs). However, as the legal duty of LEAs to make 'adequate' provision was never clearly defined, some authorities reduced or dropped this kind of provision altogether and many increased their fees to cover the costs of delivering it. This led to a reduction in less formal programmes for adults in some areas and to a decrease in participation, particularly among older adults. (See Schedule 2)

O

Office for Standards in Education (Ofsted)

Ofsted was set up on September 1992. It is a non-ministerial government department whose main aim is to improve the quality and standards of education and childcare through independent inspection and regulation, and to provide advice to the Secretary of State. The role has expanded in recent years to include reviews of local education authorities (LEAs), inspection of initial teacher-training courses, the nursery sector, schools and to report on LEA-funded youth services.

Ofsted also reports on the impact of government initiatives such as education action zones and the national numeracy and literacy strategies.

In 2001, Ofsted assumed responsibility for inspecting all education and training for ages 16-19 in sixth form and further education colleges. Through area-wide inspection reports, the overall planning of education and training provision for post-16 learners throughout England is reviewed.

Office of the Deputy Prime Minister (ODPM)

This is the Government department responsible for neighbourhood renewal, housing and urban policy. The ODPM includes the Neighbourhood Renewal Unit, the Regional Coordination Unit and the Social Exclusion Unit.

Online learning

Online learning is a type of learning organised through the Internet. The learning can be delivered using pre-prepared course materials available through the Internet, connections to the World Wide Web, email tutorial feedback and video conferencing. It is an important way of delivering open and distance learning. Currently many universities use online learning as a way of managing increased student numbers without appointing more staff.

Open and distance learning (ODL)

ODL is the term increasingly used for open and distance modes of learning which are often combined and inter-dependent, as in the case of the Open University. (See distance learning; open learning)

Open College Network (OCN)

OCNs are locally-managed, not-for-profit partnerships committed to providing a flexible and responsive local accreditation service for adults involved in a wide range of learning activities. There are currently 28 OCNs in England, Wales and

Northern Ireland. OCNs are licensed by and members of the National Open College Network (NOCN). (See National Open College Network)

Open Learning

Open learning is an independent and flexible mode of learning that enables an individual to learn at their own pace and at a time and place of their choice. This mode of learning responds to some of the barriers that prevent adults from participating in organised learning, such as time constraints and physical location. Open learning usually involves specially designed learning materials and access to support where needed, such as tutorial assistance and other supports.

Open University (OU)

The OU was established in 1971 to serve adult learners and is the foremost provider of open and distance learning. It is Britain's largest single teaching institution and the first university in the UK established to teach its students through supported open and distance learning. The OU aims to help adults overcome time and distance barriers to studying and attracts students from different social and economic backgrounds.

Output

Output is the practical and measurable elements resulting from a scheme or project. Outputs are usually measured against agreed targets and may contribute to the achievement of overall outcomes. For example, a learning output may relate to the number of people who found a job after being on a training course, whereas a learning outcome might be trainees' increases in confidence and levels of skill.

Some funding regimes, particularly statutory ones and European Social Fund, link funding levels and payments to outputs.

Output measures tend to stress things that are easily counted, i.e. numbers rather than quality.

Outreach

There is no single, universally accepted definition of 'outreach' in an educational context, and a number of meanings have accrued to the term. Most people, however, understand it as meaning work that is undertaken outside an institution to increase awareness of and participation in education among those who do not or cannot take advantage of organised learning opportunities. Understood in this way, outreach can entail both a widening participation strategy and a marketing or recruitment strategy: a process of raising awareness of the existing learning opportunities offered by local institutions and organisations and delivering some of them in community locations, often local centres established specifically for that purpose.

Outreach is also frequently defined as the development of new learning programmes tailored to the interests and requirements of specific groups and delivered in informal community locations used for other purposes, such as community centres or village halls. Some also define it as an informal and student-centred approach or style of working, or as a process of support for community groups and organisations.

P

Participation
In the post-16 educational context, participation usually refers to engagement in organised educational or training programmes.

Participatory Learning Appraisal
This approach to research and development originated in the developing world and has become increasingly useful in 'developed' (western) countries. The technique brings together a team of researchers and local practitioners to work with local people. The approach works best on tackling local issues. Local people are recognised as being experts in the issues being addressed and they define the ways in which these can be approached and resolved through the sharing of information and ideas.

Pedagogy
This refers to the principles and practice of teaching. (See androgogy.)

Performance Indicators (PIs)
PIs are criteria established to identify how well an organisation, service or particular piece of work is operating and achieving planned goals. PIs enable recognition of whether specific quality indicators and targets have been met.

Personal Development Plan (PDP)
A PDP is an agreed scheme of future activity which is drawn up in response to individual career or educational needs. (See individual learning plan.)

Positive discrimination
This refers to policies and practices which favour minority groups (for example, ethnic groups and women) who have regularly experienced disadvantages – especially in relation to work and education. In the US the sister terms 'affirmative action', 'positive action' and 'reverse discrimination' are frequently used. The advocates of

positive discrimination argue that it is a necessary corrective when it comes to securing equality of opportunity with historically privileged groups. However, this is highly controversial and has generated considerable legal and political argument.

Post-Compulsory Education/Post-16 Education
Any education which takes place after leaving school (normally at the age of 16).

Problem-based learning
Problem-based learning is an approach which attempts to encourage critical thinking by posing problems which require learners to apply knowledge and logic in order to resolve. More traditional approaches to learning tend to transmit information and knowledge which learners are expected to absorb and apply.

Progression
In an educational context, progression usually refers to the positive moves or advances learners make as a result of learning, for example moves to further learning, into employment or into active roles in the local community. The term is therefore often used to express either notions of career advancement, or progression through a hierarchy of learning levels, from one course or programme to another, usually higher level, one.

Progression is also sometimes defined as intellectual development within a subject area or discipline. However some prefer to describe this as 'progress', and to make a clear distinction between the two terms.

Progression routes
Progression routes are learning pathways people take between different levels of learning or between different learning environments. These can be created by offering gradually more advanced levels of learning in the same subject/discipline or skill area, or by providing mechanisms that help people move between different learning sectors and institutions such as advice and guidance and different forms of learner and learning support.

Protocols
These are the ground rules and operating behaviours established in order to ensure that groups and organisations work effectively and in accordance with agreed and established procedures.

Pump-priming
This is the principle of funding a project on a short-term basis in order to get it started, on the understanding that the organisation running it will then secure other funding to sustain and develop it. In reality, many innovative, educational

projects that have begaun as pump-priming activities have not subsequently been absorbed into mainstream practice when the short-term funding ended.

Qualifications
A qualification is an official record of an achievement awarded for the successful completion of an education or training course or the passing of an examination. Many qualifications are nationally recognised by the Qualifications and Curriculum Agency (QCA), for example GCSEs, A-levels, degrees, NVQs and other vocational qualifications. (See accreditation.)

Qualitative research
Qualitative research is concerned with evidence that provides an in-depth under-standing of its subject matter rather than simply facts and figures. It seeks to discover how people think and feel and why, and what their experience has been. It is complementary to quantitative research which is concerned mainly with assigning numerical properties to research findings. The most insightful research contains elements of both approaches. (See quantitative research.)

Quality assurance
This is a systematic process which uses standards of measurement to help identify what an organisation does well and what needs to be done in order to bring about improvements. Publicly funded education and training institutions are required to conform to specific standards that are monitored through a regular inspection process.

Quantitative research
This is a research approach that produces evidence that can be easily measured and presented in numbers. (See qualitative research.)

Race
This is a scientifically discredited term previously used to describe biologically distinct groups who were alleged to have genetic characteristics of an unalterable nature. Racial attributes such as skin colour, facial characteristics, size etc do not derive from differences in genetic make up. Nor does reputable scientific opinion

now claim that there are innate differences of personality, intelligence or aptitude based on these characteristics.

Race relations

This refers to the social relationships between different ethnic or racial groups in any given area. Race relations are often called upon to be improved to eliminate the effects of discrimination and racism on groups which are singled out for such treatment.

The term is controversial in that continuing use of the word 'race' lends support to the biological notion of race which has no clear scientific foundation. (See race; racialism)

Racialism or racism

Racism refers to the unequal treatment of a group on the basis of physical or other characteristics which are associated with their supposed membership of a particular 'race'. Racism is the overt and covert system of hostile and/or ignorant beliefs and attitudes which sustains racialism.

Refugees – see asylum seekers and refugees.

Regeneration

Regeneration in a social and community context refers to a process that aims to radically and comprehensively address the challenges and issues faced by people in low-income areas. It is often associated with economic, physical and environmental improvements but it also applies to strengthening and extending community organisations and networks and securing the skills and experience that enable residents to participate fully in local decision-making.

Community regeneration has been a key goal of the current government. Early schemes were often criticised for being top-down and for focusing on housing and environmental problems rather than on people-led, bottom-up regeneration. (See Neighbourhood renewal)

Regional Development Agencies (RDAs)

These are located in each of the nine English regions and they co-ordinate economic and regeneration activities. RDAs produce regional strategies to address economic development, skills and employment, regeneration and sustainable development needs of their particular region.

Revenue funding

This is the funding used to run activities, purchase consumable and small items of equipment, and pay staff and accommodation costs.

S

Schedule 2

Schedule 2 courses were those designated for direct central funding in the Further and Higher Education Act of 1992. According to the Act, accredited courses for adults and those leading to progression were to be funded directly by the Further Education Funding Council (FEFC). These included: accredited courses leading to qualifications (NVQs, GCSEs, GCE AS and A-levels); courses providing access to higher level courses in further and higher education; adult literacy and basic skills (ABE) and English for Speakers of other Languages (ESOL) and some courses for people with learning difficulties and disabilities which could show 'progression'. Other courses (non-Schedule 2) were left to local authorities to provide. The widely disliked distinction between these types of provision was removed in the Learning and Skills Act of 2000. (See non-schedule 2 courses)

Scottish Vocational Qualifications (SVQs) – see National Vocational Qualifications (NVQs).

Sector Skills Councils (SSCs)

SSCs aim to tackle the skills and productivity needs of different industry and business sectors which are economically or strategically significant. The SSCs are supported by the Sector Skills Development Agency. These industry-wide bodies are developed by groups of influential employers. They also actively involve trade unions, professional bodies and other stakeholders in their sectors. Licensed by the Department for Skills and Education each SSC aims to set targets and priorities to address four key areas. These are:

- reducing skills gaps and shortages;
- improving productivity, business and public service performance;
- increasing opportunities to boost the skills and productivity of everyone in the sector's workforce; and
- improving learning supply, including apprenticeships, higher education and national occupational standards. (See NTOs.)

Sector Skills Development Agency (SSDA)

The role of the SSDA is to support and develop sector skills councils (SSCs). Its main responsibilities are to help those bidding to become SSCs and ensure consistent standards across the network. It monitors performance across the UK and ensures that both specific and generic skill requirements are covered effectively. It also promotes the sharing of best practice and establishes common standards for all sectors. The SSDA replaces NTOs industry sectors.

Sexism
Refers to the unfair treatment and discrimination (especially in relation to women) on the basis of sex. Sexism occurs at different levels from the individual (e.g. in terms of jokes, abuse, hostility, violence) to the institutionalised (e.g. in terms of pay differentials and gendered labour markets), but all forms combine to sustain inequality.

Single Regeneration Budget (SRB)
This provides funding for partnerships of local stakeholders, usually led by a local authority, to regenerate deprived areas. The programme was set up to bring funding programmes from several government departments into one pot. There are some 600 SRB partnerships running over 9,000 schemes. The work of local regeneration partnerships is broadly based and aims to have a diverse membership which includes voluntary and community organisations.

Skilled for Health
This is a joint project launched in 2003, between The Department of Education and Skills and the Department of Health. The project aims to improve people's levels of literacy and numeracy, as well as linking learning to health. NHS patients will be able to participate in a variety of learning opportunities. Skilled for Health will help people to manage practical situations such as making an appointment with a doctor, or calculating a dosage of medicine.

Skills
Some broad skill areas have been identified:

*   Academic or cognitive skills. These are associated with subjects defined by traditional disciplines, such as English, mathematics, history and science.
*   Technical skills. These are usually defined as the specific skills required in specific occupations which may include the ability to use or operate particular tools or machinery
*   Generic skills. These are sometimes also referred to as key or core skills such as problem-solving, communications or working in teams
*   Soft skills. These usually refer to personal attributes such as confidence, assertiveness, adaptability etc

Skills Escalator

The skills escalator is an approach to supporting career potential and development across the NHS workforce. NHS employees are encouraged through lifelong learning to renew and extend their skills and knowledge to the extent of their ability so they can move up the escalator. The Skills Escalator approach is also about attracting a wider range of people to work within the NHS by offering a variety of step-on and step-off points along the continuum of education, training and personal development opportunities. (See NHSU)

Skills for Life

This is the Government's strategy for improving adult literacy and numeracy skills. The priority is to improve the skills of those groups with the greatest literacy and numeracy needs. Set up in 2001, the strategy aims to improve the literacy and numeracy skills of 750,000 adults by 2004 and to help 1.5 million people by 2007, ultimately working towards reducing the problem altogether.

Skills Strategy

The skills strategy was set out in the White paper *21st Century Skills; realising our potential* in 2003. The aim is 'to ensure that employers have the right skills to support the success of their businesses, and that individuals have the skills they need to be both employable and personally fulfilled'. [Another White Paper is to be introduced in 2005.]

SMART

This is the acronym used to describe the process of planning, setting and following through objectives and targets:

S = Specific about what is to be accomplished
M = Measurable, differences must be identified
A = Achievable, attainable targets should be established
R = Relevant, result output orientated change is desirable
T = Time-limits should be established

This process is useful to follow when planning or reviewing a project or specific parts of a project.

Social capital

Social capital refers to the collective benefit accruing from individuals being involved in social organisations, such as networks and community groups that come together and co-operate for mutual benefit. Its key constituents include social relationships, social support, group membership, shared norms, trust and community involvement. The stronger these networks and bonds, the more likely it is that members of a community will co-operate for mutual benefit and bring about collective participation in areas such as community learning and health improvements. (See cultural capital; human capital.)

Social enterprise
Social Enterprises are financially viable and sustainable businesses that trade in the market to fulfil social aims, such as employment creation or the provision of local services. They bring people and communities together for economic development and social gain and have three common characteristics of:

* being Enterprise Oriented,
* having Social Aims and
* having Social Ownership.

Social exclusion
Social exclusion is now routinely used as a social category and is a term which both describes and covers a multitude of sins. It is defined by the Social Exclusion Unit as a shorthand label for what can happen when individuals or areas suffer from a combination of linked problems such as unemployment, poor skills, low incomes, poor housing, high crime environments, bad health and family breakdown. This definition concentrates on problems that are suffered from rather like misfortunes or the symptoms of an illness. It ignores causation. The origins of the linked problems that result in social exclusion lie in deep-seated and historically based social inequalities, absolute poverty and the divisions created by social class, 'race' and gender. These are exacerbated by oppression, discrimination, exploitation and racism. Social exclusion is about more than multiple disadvantages. It is about the effects that poverty and lack of power have on people's ability to participate, or to be taken seriously by others, in society. The term is often used as a euphemism for poverty, class or racial inequality. (See social inclusion.)

Social Exclusion Unit (SEU)
The Social Exclusion Unit in the Office of the Deputy Prime Minister was set up by the Prime Minister in 1997 to help improve Government action to reduce social exclusion by producing 'joined-up solutions to joined-up problems'.

Social inclusion
Social inclusion is an attempt to address the problems which make people socially and economically excluded. To emphasise social inclusion is to seek to bring excluded groups 'in from the cold' and to 'celebrate difference and diversity' rather than discriminate against those who experience social problems or who are seen

as somehow 'different' from majority and mainstream social groups. The term is positive but tends to ignore the structural divisions and deep-seated inequalities that make simply 'celebrating diversity' problematic. The use of the term 'social inclusion' is often an attempt to put a more positive spin on the more negative connotations of social exclusion. (See social exclusion.)

Socrates
This is the European Commission's action programme in the field of education of which Grundvig is a part. Involving around 30 European countries. Its objectives are to promote lifelong learning, encourage access to education for everybody and to help people acquire recognised qualifications and skills. (See Grundvig.)

Soft outcomes
Soft outcomes are the outcomes of learning that are not easily quantifiable or open to rigorous scrutiny. These may include soft skills, such as the ability to work with others, problem-solving and negotiation skills. They also include personal qualities, such as increased confidence and self-esteem, motivation, acknowledging and managing feelings and being self-aware, as well as determination and a willingness to learn. (See hard outcomes)

Stakeholders
These are individuals or organisations with a special interest in an organisation, project, service or issue. Stakeholders in a voluntary organisation include management committee members, other volunteers, staff, and users of the service, funders, customers, suppliers, and neighbours in the community. The stakeholders in post-16 education would include funders, managers, staff and learners themselves (and if publicly-funded, the public as a whole).

Steering groups
Steering groups are appointed to guide the progress of individual research or development projects. The group meets less regularly than the management group and has membership drawn from the wider community and network representatives of the project. It makes recommendations to the project, receives information on progress and feeds back information on the effectiveness of the work. Members contribute to wider evaluation questions and can help in sustaining strands of work after the project is over.

Strategic Area Reviews (StARS)
StARS were started in April 2003 to ensure that learners in each part of the country have high quality, safe and accessible learning opportunities capable of meeting their needs and those of employers and local communities. In carrying out the

reviews, Local Learning and Skills Councils, Local Authorities, Jobcentre Plus, learners, employers, communities, schools, colleges and other providers to ensure that provision is well planned.

Strategic planning
Strategic planning concentrates on the steps a group, an organisation or particular piece of work, needs to take to achieve identified goals.

Student-centred learning/student-centred approach
This is a way of approaching learning and teaching that emphasises student participation in all processes of adult learning including planning and delivery of learning, negotiating the curriculum and evaluation. A student-centred approach is particularly characteristic of non-accredited and community based adult education. (See learner-centred learning)

Study circles
Study circles represent an emancipatory and participatory approach to learning. They are based on a group – study circles – meeting informally over a period of time to discuss and learn together. The person who leads the study group acts as a facilitator rather than a teacher. The approach aims to be empowering and democratic. Study circles originated in and are popular as a form of learning in Nordic countries.

Success for All
The DfES White Paper *Success for All: reforming further education and training* (2002) sets out the government's overarching strategy for reforming further education and training. The overall aim is to raise standards and increase coherence in post-16 provision. The strategy encourages providers to review and define their missions. The Paper also heralded the introduction of Strategic Area Reviews.

Summative evaluation
This form of evaluation takes place on completion of a programme and evaluates a project's or learner's performance and progress as a whole. Summative evaluations of projects may be used to inform future practice but are carried out at a point which cannot impact on the existing practice of the project. (See Formative evaluation.)

Sure Start
Sure Start is one of a range of government policy initiatives that was developed from cross-departmental reviews of services for children and young people. It was established to provide a cross-sector initiative involving health, education, social

services and parents in providing more integrated, joined-up services for children aged 0-4, their parents and families. Sure Start focuses on achieving better access to childcare, health services, support for parents and children's education. In adult and community learning, family learning programmes are frequently attached to the Sure Start initiative.

Surface learning

Surface learning refers to rote learning or learning by heart for the purpose of passing an assessment or examination. It does not involve in-depth learning and may not lead to true understanding of the subject being learnt.

Sustainability

Sustainability means ensuring that a project or scheme continues in one form or another when funding ends. For example, regeneration schemes seek to ensure that improvements are sustainable beyond the end of the funding or investment that they make. This means equipping people, projects, organisations and communities with the necessary resources, knowledge, commitment, and skills that can contribute to preserving initiatives and enhancing developments so that they can be continued into the future.

Funders often want evidence that a project is sustainable. This means they want to know how the project will be resourced and continued once their money comes to an end.

Sustainable development

This is an approach which seeks to ensure that present needs are met while ensuring that future generations will also be able to meet their needs. This approach takes full account of the social, economic and environmental impacts of decisions over the long-term by ensuring that developments recognise population needs, protecting the environment and using resources carefully. The aim is to ensure a better quality of life for everyone now, and for the generations to come.

SWOT

SWOT is an acronym which stands for Strengths, Weaknesses, Opportunities and Threats. It is a method used for reflecting upon and focusing attention on systems and strategies within an organisation in a way that seeks to improve performance.

Synchronous learning

Synchronous learning is a real-time, instructor-led online learning event in which all participants are logged on at the same time and communicate directly with each other. The instructor leads the learning and maintains integrated classroom control, with the ability to call on participants who raise their electronic hands from a distant location. Students and teachers use a whiteboard to see work in progress and share knowledge. Content can be delivered using live online courses (virtual classroom), audio/video conferencing, and two-way live broadcasts of lectures to students in a classroom.

T

Taster sessions
These are short, one-off opportunities designed to give people a 'taste' of what a course or programme entails and enable potential learners to try something new. They are a device frequently used by colleges and other providers to encourage new students to enrol for courses.

Third Age
The 1993 *Carnegie Inquiry into the Third Age* defined the Third Age as a stage of life between 50-75 years. The period post 75 is frequently referred to as the Fourth Age. In a climate in which the focus of the governments learning and skills policy is directed towards younger age groups, especially in relation to training for and participation in the labour market, the learning needs of older learners are frequently marginalized. This should be of concern given the demographic trend towards an ageing society.

Third sector
Voluntary organisations, community groups and other non-profit organisations are sometimes referred to as the third sector because they are not part of the public or private sectors. The term is often used instead of the voluntary sector which can be misleading as it can be understood as a sector comprised of volunteers.

Tokenism
Tokenism refers to the practice of doing the minimum (sometimes in a rather cynical way) to comply with a directive or requirement. For example, a token response to increasing democratic participation and consultation in a learning organisation would involve adding a learner representative to a committee or advisory group in circumstances in which the individual learner has little power or influence. Some groups and committees would claim to be complying with equal opportunities practice by including a 'token' member of a black or ethnic minority group or a 'token' member with a disability.

Transferable skills

Skills gained in one setting that can be applied in another. For example, individuals can acquire communication, organisational and other skills at home or in voluntary settings, which they can then apply in a paid work situation. The development of schemes to assess or accredit prior experiential learning is based on the recognition that many people have acquired a range of skills informally, although they have not been formally learnt and assessed. (See accreditation of prior experiential learning; accreditation of prior learning)

U

UK Online Centres

The centres were established in 2000 and were designed to provide convenient access to the internet and e-mail. They are located in venues such as Internet Cafés, public libraries, colleges, community centres or other suitable locations. UK Online Centres are intended to help develop Internet skills to access information and send emails. They can also be used to access further learning opportunities. (See Learning centres)

University for Industry Limited (Ufi limited)

Ufi limited is a company with charitable status concerned to boost the competitiveness of business and the employability of individuals. It offers mainly work-based courses through distance learning, especially e-learning. The use of modern technologies enables people to participate in learning at their own pace and at a suitable time and place. This includes the home, the workplace and through a national network of Learndirect centres. (See Learndirect)

University of the Third Age (U3A)

The U3A was established in France and is active in the UK as an independent voluntary organisation. It operates as a learning co-operative in which older people themselves pass on their knowledge and skills.

V

Validation
This is the process by which a course is judged to have met the requirements for providing an award by a relevant awarding body.

Video conferencing
Video conferencing is a communications medium used for lectures, tutorials, workshops, project reviews and remote site visits. A videoconference can be either two way (point-to-point) or multipoint, linking three or more sites with sound and video in real time. The most common use for videoconferencing in education is remote lectures delivered from one site to another.

Vocational education
Vocational education is training and learning that relates to an individual's current or future employment, often resulting in a qualification. Historically a distinction was frequently made between academic and vocational education, with the implication that academic education was superior. In a climate in which learning and skills for the labour market are a key government priority, the importance of vocational education – with both academic and applied dimensions – is now more widely recognised. (See National Vocational Qualifications.)

Voluntary organisation
Voluntary organisations are not-for-profit organisations of varying sizes managed by a voluntary management committee and usually employing paid staff. They may have volunteers carrying out some functions and may be charitable in their aims. They may or may not have local people and/or service users on their management committee.

Voluntary sector – see Third sector.

W

Widening participation
Although concern with opening up learning opportunities to wider sections of the community is not a new phenomenon, 'widening participation' is a relatively recent term that started to be used increasingly in the 1990s, reflecting concern that the

socio-economic profile of those engaging in organised education and training had remained largely unchanged for some decades.

The influential Kennedy report *Learning Works: Widening participation in further education* (1997, *Further Education Funding Council*) defined widening participation as *'a broad and inclusive process incorporating stages such as access, achievement and progression for those groups often under-represented in further education'*. This definition was adopted by the former Further Education Funding Council (which has now been replaced by the Learning and Skills Council).

However many providers interpret the term more narrowly, viewing widening participation largely as an *access* process designed to make the student cohort more representative of the communities served. Thus most widening participation strategies tend to involve recruitment strategies (outreach development work, provision of information and advice, curriculum development, delivery of provision in local venues and (in higher education) more flexible entry criteria). Some feel that, though essential, such strategies do not take sufficient account of institutional change which, it is argued, is necessary to widen participation in a broader sense by making institutional environments, processes and practices more responsive to a more diverse body of students.

Wider benefits of learning

Wider benefits of learning refers to those aspects of learning which cannot be measured by a credit or a qualification, such as increases in self-esteem and confidence or improved social or personal skills. Problems arise when it comes to demonstrating the value of intangible or 'soft outcomes' of learning to policymakers and funders. (See soft outcomes)

Wider Benefits of Learning Research Centre

The Wider Benefits of Learning Research Centre is funded by the DfES and based in at the Institute of Education in London, is specifically concerned with identifying and demonstrating the significance of the wider benefits of learning. (See soft outcomes.)

Work-based learning

Work-based learning is the term used to describe learning that takes place whilst a person is in employment. It includes: any learning at work, training and development of employees in the work place, on-the-job learning and learning for the work-place which is delivered on or off site. The training is usually based on individual's career needs and an employer's requirement for skilled workers.

Work-based learning can be informal and unstructured. As a result, it is not always easily measured.

Worker's Educational Association (WEA)
The WEA is the largest national voluntary provider of adult education in the UK. It is committed to providing access to education and learning for adults from all backgrounds, and in particular those who have previously missed out on education. The WEA operates at local, regional and national levels. Courses are created and delivered in response to local need, often in partnership with local community groups and organisations.

Workforce development is a strategy designed to provide training activities and learning opportunities intended to increase the participation and enhance the skills of workers in the labour market.